they will kill you if they see you so you mustn't let them see you
they will kill you if they see you so you mustn't let them see you
they will kill you if they see you so you mustn't let them see you
they will kill you if they see you so you mustn't let them see you
they will kill you if they see you so you mustn't let them see you
they will kill you if they see you so you mustn't let them see you
they will kill you if they see you so you mustn't let them see you
they will kill you if they see you so you mustn't let them see you
they will kill you if they see you so you mustn't let them see you
they will kill you if they see you so you mustn't let them see you
they will kill you if they see you so you mustn't let them see you
they will kill you if they see you so you mustn't let them see you
they will kill you if they see you so you mustn't let them see you
they will kill you if they see you so you mustn't let them see you
they will kill you if they see you so you mustn't let them see you
they will kill you if they see you so you mustn't let them see you
they will kill you if they see you so you mustn't let them see you
they will kill you if they see you so you mustn't let them see you
they will kill you if they see you so you mustn't let them see you
they will kill you if they see you so you mustn't let them see you
they will kill you if they see you so you mustn't let them see you
they will kill you if they see you so you mustn't let them see you

ISAAC PICKELL

IT'S NOT OVER ONCE YOU FIGURE IT OUT

It's not over once you figure it out

by Isaac Pickell

Black Ocean
Boston · Chicago

Black Ocean
P.O. Box 52030
Boston, MA 02205
blackocean.org

Cover Art and Design by Janaka Stucky | janakastucky.com
Book Design by Taylor D. Waring |taylordwaring.com

ISBN: 9781939568632
Library of Congress Control Number: 2023938280

FIRST EDITION

PRINTED CANADA

CONTENTS

"to name something is to wait for it
in the place you think it will pass"
 —Amiri Baraka

"but there is no proof but proof."
 —Danez Smith

THINGS YOU OUGHT TO TAKE
SITTING DOWN

they tell us to just hang
in there and even

though we're all born
with a handle we are not

all born with a string.

QUADROON

black lives are extra credit for history repeating it
self protesting changed lanes intersecting strange
fruits deep-seated with diminishing relevance
beyond lines of curriculum still buried and rooted
in compliance and community all those insider
languages peeling off master tongues you bought
with his dollar loaned at better interest than the
homeowners you can't call brother in the wrong
neighborhood where stars don't come out it stays
dark and you won't find cover for your black life
extra credit assigned to tilt the curve of mother's
pride which held your pale silhouette against the
bleached white world that must have settled her
ovum where helixes were warping grandfather's
lips into a truth that reads too horrible or boring
to be spoken. how lucky you are to be some
body's prisoner:

stitched into your side where she makes sugar pie and wears black eyes you've been spared from that morning on when you blended right in with hospital walls whose biohazard boxes disposed of all important information pertaining to history you keep claiming a generation split from Detroit City where blackface is just a birthright but black lies are extra credit for every warm embrace of miscegenation that grows between rows unspoken in family albums stiff with scar tissue on fingers and palms pressed against the corners of one room quarters muffling screams that paid for the thinnest of noses and that damn good hair the barber disposed of before another young man saw the tawny curls as black

life costing extra when his own mother tells him stop using the word oppression when you've never known its price and can't fix the cost in creases on her wrist and ankle where the skin is light and taut but the message is thankless reminders to the world her patience for fighting is aging. all she can say is don't live a dim life just be-cause you were lucky enough to be born so bright.

are for it self changed lanes with relevance under of curriculum and rooted in accommodation and all that insider from a you with his with better than the homeowners you in the where stars don't come out it and you find for your assigned to tilt the of which your silhouette against the that must have her ovum where were into a that too or boring to be spoken you are to be into your side where she makes pie and you were that morning on when you blended right in with whose biohazard of all important information to a you a generation where is a but are extra credit for every of that between in with on and against the of the that the of and that damn the barber before another young man another young man another young man another young man could see the tawny curls as when his own tells him the word when you've its and fix the in on and ankle where the is and but the is to the her patience for fighting is all can is a dim just because you were lucky enough to be born so bright

are for it self with of and in and all that from a you with his
with than the you in the where it and you for your to the of
which your the that her where were into a that too or to be you
are to be into your where she and you were that on when you
in with whose of to a you a where is a but are for of that in with
on and the of the that the of and that the before another young
man another young man another young man another young
man the as when his own him the when you've its and the in
on and where the is and but the is to the her for is a you were
to be born so bright

another young man another young man another young man
born so bright

WHAT WORDS WON'T PUT ME IN
THE GROUND

if black were human
it would be already

if you were breathing
you would be ready

for all of their bark,
if opinions were just

like assholes after all
& not the trap

doors into our dying box,
if brown were human

it would already be
clear there was not

enough for everyone,
& that not enough

was the problem
& not all of us,

scared white as human
after being reminded:

if human were enough
it would be already.

THE SLAVE WHO DISCOVERED
NEW MEXICO

Most archives will claim he came from
Morocco, but that was not a name yet;
he was not from anywhere. He was sold

> *and his skin was*
> > *said to shimmer*
> *as brushed leather was*
> > *pronounced arabized*
> > *black, was brown*

to Spanish royalty with eyes too big
for the ocean. Estevanico followed
because years earlier he discovered
chains, then Catholicism, discovered
boat hulls the size of villages, dis-
covered the hesitant sleep of the sea-
sick, discovered the good master who
pronounced him as his right hand,
whose name was not really Little
Stephen, the discoverer of the new
Mexico, resting behind museum glass.

[The expedition boasted hundreds of men meant to
colonize and plunder Florida's gulf coast; they did
not bring a single woman because Florida has no a
gold, and the men would need something to plunder.]

Florida had no gold or grazelands and so Dorantes'
Stephen followed along the coastline in early fall
and discovered the gulf hurricane that swept him
into bondage with his good master by a nameless
tribe living on Texas' Barrier Islands where he dis-
covered white genocide in Texas' standardized
history curriculum. Dorantes' Stephen was one of
four men who escaped along with good Dorantes
who followed his Stephen out into the west. Freely,

>   *everyone has survived*
> *some things that are not*
> *meant to happen, to anyone*

Black Stephen discovered the famous sky city Acoma
but was not the one who tarred its name under voices
with sails full of letters. Trusted now to walk upright,
to scale the mesas, to report back the pueblitos' fear,
Black Stephen knew Acoma was not a name yet; Black
Stephen discovered nowhere but the magic of ruins

>   *how they begin*
>   *to resemble the land*
>   *robbed in creation*

as Mustafa Zemmouri gained the trust of his fellow survivors who gained the trust of the natives who crowned them all as medicine men; he led thousands as if on a pilgrimage, their guide and their wake, from village to village, peaceful explorers trading sandstone for treasure. Across the desert,

[Mustafa Zemmouri, like Morocco, is description and not name: "Chosen Moor" creoled beyond recognition. With guns long lost, the three Spaniards followed behind his spear for the tribes they met pronounced his skin as death.]

Mustafa Zemmouri hunted for rumor. Painted in white chalk and feathers he commanded disciples to wrap sinew around sticks to carry back to the Spaniards, retracing his steps with a cross whose size corresponded to the weight of the fortune ahead. At Pueblo Cibola, his runner delivered a severed gourd; Mustafa was dead

[Cibola was a description and not a name, a forgotten Spanish word for the buffalo. Unlike the slave who discovered a new Mexico, this true name has not been lost: Hawikuh was the first pueblo conquered by the Spanish and their first failure of public relations saw adobes razed and forgotten in favor of a church. We're asked sometimes if love is possible under conditions of slavery: my mother is from somewhere and my father tarred over her name and her history, his voice full of letters and still she loves him enough. When she dies the clouds will know it.]

Some say that Estevanico faked his death to
escape love under the conditions of slavery,
that his Puebloan shadows loved enough to
risk retribution and hid him atop the mesas,
that his sons would become the first maroons
with their skin that was brown and was red,
that his life is legend, a great black ogre
scouting for Death with yellow, arabized
eyes, that his true name is Chakwaina—but
Estevanico was a medicine man whose skin
shimmered as brushed leather and bore the
cross before his body was traded for a gourd

> *like clouds that follow*
> > *storms, swollen*
> *but refusing to drop.*
> > *heavy and dark and leaving,*

we'll need more roots, soon
as the sky dries.

WHY I BUY MY CORN IN THE FREEZER AISLE

what i used to love about corn on the cob is the satisfying
control eating it up, bursting little rows in sequence like

a typewriter before i lost touch with the comfort of messes,
just outside the reach of memory. i wish i could recall

where it got left at. back there. to a child, even the cold
can be a hero because it leaves with the morning but keeps

its promises, returning every night to the people used
to waiting their turn. like the deep-blue grand-father

i never knew from the sea, his deep-blue resounding voice
i never heard who's hiding in the unkempt canopy of a shade

tree, the kind that was planted after all the others were
cut down, all of them & all of us & all our children cut down

to size so someone could choose where to put new ones right
where they offered the most shade & a good place to hang.

this whole country was built on the back of nothing so much
as vague certainty like maybe someday this'll be the land

where people chase their dreams. but you don't need to
squint through cold sunrise glare or cold twilight gloom

to see how silly that seems. we're not at the gears of anything,
let alone ourselves. there's always someone else manning

the switch, holding the skewer. so now my cobs feel messy,
like plunging both hands blindly into earth, reaching

& risking hazards like dirty & unknown. what i want is
trimmed & cleaned, shaved off pieces of roots like you

find in a dead kin's closet or wrench from under saplings
planted in the thawed ground their last spring, just a promise

of a tree before it's cut down before it's pieces before
it's a box at the end of too long a procession full of

laughter & the grin reward for lived life. for staying alive:
look out for the ones who keep laughing through yellow

teeth & a jukebox kept loose through patience and a fist, and
hear their exhale: why brace against what's natural as

it's coming: it's just the cold; breathe open, it's almost home.

NAME/BRAND

on a windy day breaking
those hottest Midwestern months

where most everything is
wishing for death

or winter, a single dried petal
from that little blue flower

with a cute colloquial name,
shrunk beyond its living

weight and crumbled a bit
on its edges, falls

from somewhere that is not
knowable to the backseat of your car

in a park, the kind with trees
and paths but not a path

through the trees, surrounded
by city and city

and suburb and trees and
something catches your eyes

in the sparse canopy. your whole
body follows until one is

captured and cataloged
by a benevolent satellite employed of a science

repeating, "When's the last time you heard Michael Brown?"

another name

to echo, to rhyme

ALL OUR MOTHERS LIVE
THROUGH THE SAME CITY BUT
THEN AGAIN THEY DIDN'T

Every day on the drive
into the city we talk

about what has happened
to [our] city and on

the drive back out
we talk about the day,

drowning in basic comforts.
Today I was those people

praying for the motor to kick
back into Highland Park
but misery isn't a place, even

if some prefer the company
to nothing at all. It's an elephant.

You're not supposed to name it.
We're busy making another great

flood: I hope I live long enough to see
the birth of fable, comforted as I am

by stubbornnesses bigger than me
as anything that size succumbs

so slowly: in Detroit, [our] famous home-
grown department store filled a sky-
scraper, then they furnished the building

with explosives and surrounded it
with bulldozers & people openly wept

over the streets, others applauded and laughed
here comes the neighborhood, all claimed the same star:

even Venus and Mars are only faking stasis,
Mars moving away from the sun and Venus

slowly returning to her: eventually your name
and your town may no longer share an orbit

but that takes a very long time: eventually, all
these rocks will be swallowed by the same fire
so carve captions into what's yours to keep them

accessible. Memory comes with traces,
poltergeists of what we made and what

we make [our] burden together on one blank
page in a book we claimed to know

the end of. Only old futures haven't been:
the decay of indecision is, maybe,

a better decay than the other sorts,
than smashing yourself again until

you are whole. So here comes
the neighborhood, the malaise of close-
cropped neon green lawns, just so.

IT DOESN'T MATTER WHO
STARTED IT

saw my house burn and then the wind
come up, saw smells of the overhanging
branches and fury and siren and diesel
fuel, and as heat rises all I could handle

was the ringing question: is that all
there is to a fire. a streak of nothing
but blurred red and the prophecy
of smolder. of unsalted earth, fertile

for the fallen structure, for the loss
of sharp corners and careful edging,
for the ignorance of kitchen islands,
security systems, bay windows, smart

home. just memory of brick and birch.
some days, you can't be the delicate
gardener, maintainer of bulb and root.
some days you only find the clawed foot:

the water's smoke, the child's choked.
when your house burns in a rising wind
you start planting trees for eyes that won't
know our mess, who haven't opened yet.

Yours will be a future
without a future
already in ruins

THE FUTURE IS NOT AN OPTION

there is so much beauty
& cruelty & we have

not imagined
the half of it. out there

        are words
for dreams

so vivid I wake feeling
like I've left them

somewhere, for the end
        of constant linger.

the chattering class endures on
succor & intention, denying

        that right

now people are dying
who've never died before

with just enough
beauty left to keep us

never asking after
the other half

who can proudly lie:
the moon does nothing

    I feel on my skin.

WE ARE MORE THAN MERE ENDURANCE

What I love about ruins
is how they begin
to resemble the land

robbed in creation:
another infant rooting
just above strata

that remembers how
smoothly thunder hushed us
to sleep, like we have

evolved to drift and slumber
whenever the sky portends
danger, as if I were talking

to myself and taking off
my clothes to be closer
to the dirt; making snow shadows

in the playground,
time takes shape painlessly
about me. I laid in the middle

of streets at night,
walked through town
making stories of the people

in their beds,
telling whole stories
in a flurry of blurred reminiscence

with ourselves at the center, cowering
from the helpless terror of being
just one person. But the math

for empathy isn't supposed to add up
I say to my body, softly,

WE ARE ALL LIVING FICTION

It never occurred
to me to open

the window, the hell
would I want

with the sky?
The sky's stuck
in last year's snow

or something else
soft to sink into;
maybe we'd sound

soft enough on another
planet—finding yourself

a repository for all those
things that can't be killed.

I trust near misses
more than wounds, how

no one understands "no"
is a full sentence
& someday you will

turn seventy-seven
even if you die first
& even then not

a day will pass
when you don't

break something
for the first time.

you

resist,

defining

struggle

by

yourself.

our

fragility

made

flesh

from

[   ]

against

the

concrete

the

present,

remaining

naïve

critic

of

the
                                                    future,

written

futures, within

                              the

          already

                                        has

          been.

horizons

forget

we, too

are

quick

to

recede,

always,

only

&

that

I've always been drawn to the aging process of our immobile
Objects & the stories behind them, like a still locomotive
Corroding where we left it, like fences growing into trees.
I like to think our things are travelers that precede and then
Follow us, getting lost and found and in between finding
Deep dark places no one cares or dares to look. A truth
Uncovered by its permanence. I wonder, if we become things,
What do we find? Maybe our future will be settled in the Rust
Belt, as if that could be a place and not a description, as if
Immobile objects age or die or have stories we did not write
Ourselves. But this is just a poem, where you are allowed
To write literally whatever you want to: like how this is not settling
Anything at all, like how our dreams can do better than doubt,
Which is not growth, like how self-awareness is no finish line.

TO GRASP IT SELF

it's hard to capture the life
you live, even to imagine it

all at once is lonely; the lights are
so bright and you can be a reflection

or you can be a mirror, but deference
to some other higher purveyor of choice

leaves you as no more than muslin
membrane, woven into the story

only to be seen

through. there is no right way to capture
a life, only knowing or knowing, too much.

UNCOMMISSIONED ELEGY FOR
THE CHILDREN OF CHILDREN

The world is dying but so
are we, hothouse flowers: how weird

that everything there is is
somebody's job. Let us pollinate

your lore. That's the thing
about the world: it's terrible

but so good, with all of this
& nowhere left to set

one's feet. We could look
so pretty outside: liberty, still

that very bitter joke; the colors

only fade when you are
convinced of such a thing

as original shade; how weird
that everything there was was

somebody's job. There's no
shame, dying for nothing.

there is a man in an alley who looks to either side
before meeting your eyes he is selling matches for
a dollar a stick in front of him is a little hole no
wider than your hips it echoes when you look he'll
light the match for no extra charge and gestures to
the scarred ground promising full cabinets for your
children only the driest of tears you'll feel better
once you're through another you hands him a
dollar and watches the echoes drowned out by the
sounds of a thousand people screaming for their
lives there is one more hole you must not have
seen no wider than your fist that starts to gurgle
with smoke you turn to the man and see that it will
grow into a geyser. you ask the man "who is down
there and what is happening to them" "I don't
know" and he hands back your dollar

holding nothing, but shuttered and still standing
proud with palm on elbow and palm on elbow
held tight by too many nails—debt to the man who
made you promise never to take anything:

from a funeral, not your
bread or flour not even
flowers not even candy

so you will not be brushed or dusted into rows cut
from your roots & your dirt is still supple when the
sun is replaced by winter you will not be processed and
stripped and bleached and quality checked you will not
be filtered through the finest mesh leaving most of you
behind & no. No, you will not be bottled you will not
be sold as a drink with

a pulse. sit the dark until the sun comes, dream about
the places that make you nostalgic let history decide
what did or did not happen.

TO WRITE POETRY AFTER THE WORLD BURNS IS BARBARIC BUT THE WORLD IS STILL BURNING

what a lie
what nonsense, fear moves
plenty of mountains—

I sit waiting for my hands
to become breathing

& blinking things. How absurd
to talk about yourself but you must

in degrees of extension,
as anyone who can hold

you can erase you—
which is true & not true,

      like there is no from
      & there is no to.

how far is a flower drawn, bending
itself close to a picture

of familiar & absent sun—
how long must you work

before your hands become
unrecognizable—how hollow

the mountains that never
ever wear us?

DECAY:RELAY

so cause problems
with purpose for the enemy's

entropy, like: if people only knew
this is a mess no one intends to clean

or that problems without solutions are really problems
with solutions that only help

to the kind of people they pronounce
they or them or you

know who, can you even imagine,
all those billions

in property damage if it were compulsory
to name how long they've made the same

indecisions with no better reason but to keep
making more of them. this whole thing is closing in

on the brink: it's either collapse or break us
into constituent molecules.

but their ends are not disorder,
or chaos. the truth of it is

there was always already a natural order
& it's beautiful & we're a part of it.

the world we've been bent to build in
their image could be shaped by another

model; this one's only carved in stone
because the wrong people keep finding chisels.

we too can rise dusty up mountaintops
& won't need make believe to say

something caught fire. Your life
should not need to be

politics, but it is; your breath
should not need to escape

but they've bought every
dictionary & sealed every

word that still feels
like a present worth fighting for

behind labels—vulgar or archaic.
if we don't break it,

we'll be replaced by soft & lethal
composite fibers only

cops & landlords know
where to buy. but the past is

what you make of it & the future,
the future does not need

to echo anything
to be heard:

it's okay or it is

gonna be ok.

IN THE ABSENCE OF A PARROT

airbrushed past all recognition
of our predation, still rises a shadow

at the whole of us which word alone
cannot erase from the geologic record

expanding as we are into time measured
in strata, the historical record keeps

the familiar shapes of our noses, the color
on our backs and our shoulders, the voices
trapped as legacies of legacy invested in ornaments

like truth, molded into anachronistic
oddities waiting for their day to be

sold at a market literate in the value of remains
grown small with time, even our oak shriveled, softened

for the hands of children elastic as they wiggle
the rods, rattle bladeless sabers, able to imagine
they never sought blood, never drained color from any face

recognizable as man; how inviting these artifacts are
as they approach dissolution. even waves turn
static waiting for break, distance decays, even

the sand slows itself from melting as glass resting
between you and drowning, an imagined protection

expanding as we are into time measured
in strata, the historical record keeps

a hilly cemetery nearby in the tall weightless grass, an old
barn melting into ground across the bay, a good place
to share with a cat or something else to outlive, accessories

to remember instead of leaving behind. the world at my back,
exposed to nothing but the humming drone of nothing, the rest
of the world all in process. become this thing we tell ourselves we are

expanding as we are into time measured
in strata, the historical record keeps

the grief that your cat lacks when it fails
to miss you, or your own

nostalgia, an evolutionary wedge that found a way
to process loss as promise, holding on

to every one of our mistakes, until mirrors
fade back into sand and we drown

under the weight of it all

the historical record keeps
for its sheer number of things

expanding as we are, the time
to answer questions is past.

NO, WE CANNOT WEEP TOGETHER

in the absence of a parrot,
    who is left say: to death,

to fear; to our society of the spectacle
    where the global south is mythic
        until you accept there is no magic

to airplanes, where slums below are only
    a premise to rename what is closest to you
        as far away; to an evil that's just banal

replacement for sensation as need is already
    a full-time job; to absorption of the globe's
        breaks, only ever a named a frame

when language acts become grandstanding;
    when blitz can be read as dance and tactic
        and song, another misheard fare;

to every extant text inflicted on the sprawling
    hillsides we have dotted with low hanging
        mimesis, clouding the master narrative

that is our narrative: we're arriving at late stage
        everything, this system only one victim,
                demanding justice for the plastic bags

the garbage flotilla in the pacific ocean
        the lives that are made into matter
                the fires that still thirst for

the huddled masses getting ever more massive
        the standards of political discourse
                the distance between west and south

the economy of the shared sonoran
        desert the women we can't trace with other women
                like maquiladoras who remain inexpendably

widgeted: there are other forms of possession
        for some of us; this is no time
                to blink from the page.

YOU WILL PAY FOR YOUR OSMOSIS
& IT WILL MAKE YOU SMILE

So many true things sound
fantastic when transposed
to the west, to our present,
to the soothing associations

we grant the English language,
the heroic civility of our
frustration, calls to action
patiently waiting on generations

to monetize them, to our catch
phrases masquerading as
vernacular, to our tshirts,
all our fucking tshirts, stiff

black text over white
cotton or black behind
softer white words, the way
labor is spelled the same

whether it comes before
power or camp, if not
to our mutiny at least
to our comfort where

there is time to memorize
the refrain: am I making
something or am I reiterating
the idea of myself. We chant

just below a mutual
detection so that one
cannot hear the other's
effacements never meant

for answers but to lay bare
better questions: you'll never
grow big and strong or
tender or mild without

learning to appreciate
what we can't understand:

the object cannot explain
the walls built around her

even as they wilt against
the grease on our fingers

toward an irreparable humanity
now too powerful to resist

now recognizable as the same
boots they have always been &

when you meet the hologram
and give it a name you lose

faith in everything but the buoy
of writing ourselves in human.

UNCOMMISSIONED ELEGY
AND THE BODY

The first digital corpse traded
pain for posterity, taking poison
rejecting its rightful chair—

but the audience, applause,
audience forever inside
your drive, he is saved—

he dies for endless dissection
consonant with the expectation
we are allowed to linger on

the skin of a criminal, repeating
hierarchies of the global organ:
the first visible man relives his

American Dream on knees
bending every way, plastic
collapse, all ribs and earlobes

FOR JOSEPH PAUL JERNIGAN
OF MICHAEL BROWN

every piece of your body,
that keeps growing even after
you fall into bare bones

horizon reseeding into digital
morgues renaming the mortuary
a science, a clinical gaze,

determining who is human by coordinates
for who was, plotted with rulers, clamps
and forceps, splayed onto touch

screens: the body is now swiped through.
Now you can refresh us, refresh, refresh,
update until we are cross-sections,

millimeter by millimeter, softened
enough as slivers of data until we are
made to matter, reassorted into the new

archive. Those photographs
were never really surgeons,

once freeze-framed and still
life, close-up, invisibly

projecting us as larvae, fat and full
on promised knowledge, category
our new chrysalis: like the butterflies

bloom, not knowing they used to be
goo that can hold onto memory,
wormy smells of fear and hope

and safety—now we are
freed, unpeeling crispy

layers off binary wings,
promises to disseminate

as truth over myth, even in death.
And so what if we lose our fleshy
interior, separate from muscle. Untether

[This poem is a stereoscope.]

from every embedded response
metamorphing all our skin cells

in a flash, excluded life exposed
as a toolbox. The corpse

of the future sees everyone resting
in digital desk drawers, writing

free obituaries each day as another
cover for autopsy in the background

awaiting the prize of our so-called moment
of death: how quickly do you erase the body

under the sheets where it finally rested:
remember: yours is not the first corpse to be
come glamour
dazzle

with that soft pink matter.

look, no one said butterflies could—
no butterfly ever asked to be
a metaphor for flowering thought—

look, here!
        ~no one really tells the butterflies shit.

THE STORIES THAT AREN'T (TOLD)

a psalm

she said there's nothing about us
without us, dissolution as in:
stagnation, intransigence in black
life, pure force undiluted by
reparation, an unfamilial beauty
indebted to pale reflections whose
possibility for neutral remains
undiagnosed: it's too easy to say
white is neutral, splintered i-
dentities and emergent modes re:
defining oppression as a poetry
prompt, free use and always fair
trade, leaving only the purposeful
discontents disconnected. black

is not neutral, the shape of the back of
my head is not neutral, the ways mother
names each of her grandparents in the blur:
red quadrants where my hair grows against
its best interests are not neutral, questioning
when I should apply what product, blackness applied
to that part behind your cowlicks, isn't that funny:
I don't see a lot of regular people with hair like that an:

other forms of mimicry: can caricature resist
the smooth charcoal scratches darkening our own
outlines as [prerecorded bodies painted by ex:
pensive pencils rosying the cheeks of toy soldiers] mimicry,

are prerecorded bodies, [mimicry]
are masks, [mimicry] are pressed onto
postcards and offered free for museum
opening weekends, [mimicry] are now available
for purchase, [mimicry] are silhouettes of enslaved
people with intimate trans-Atlantic travel plans and
[mimicry] dreams of the rising white pillar of Washington's
promise he never really made & you can't help but see when leaving
the gift shop where you're told all proceeds contribute to curating

the archives are [mimicry], assumptions my body will be
curated, mocked in blank blue screens after presentation
endings. read close enough every white text about black
text feels guilty for the open ocean, my white texts over
black text until the water remembers its blue only for
recreation, the earliest paintings, how poorly captured
live bodies project onto prerecorded bodies in the complex:
ions of masks I wear: what does my body feel when it touches
skin: outrageously magical things happen, when you play around
without the semblance of a symbol:

discourse! the provenance of whiteness deserves more
working through, demands reprocessing language
past thought into instinct into the common idea:
logical heritages of man into every good philosopher
must contend with King Kunta and his Black Jesus
hanging in the hut, framed with the switches grand:
mother found behind the great house into the Other

should be capitalized: like every retelling of Icarus
performed as homage to ancestors
drowning, unable to afford a plane ticket.

but Icarus need not be a cautionary tale. learning
to read demands we draw very close to its
light, eyes and skin acclimate to abduction, all
our gods' children can have wings; in youth's
speculative poetics, line breaks don't fall into the sea.

But in my hands, what becomes of the oldest myths?
Can they stack or pool or bend, do they pass

between bodies, slip through fingers, soothe
in slippage, break into creases, accelerate through

opacity, through divination, through
the inevitability of warping what's left in common:

we are stoic, not silenced; we are laying lucidity
to rest; we are buying stock in the intractable Other

printed in the same weight and shade
as the half-height walls that kept us

a part and the rounded hull, smooth
and human and meant for a return

voyage we weren't offered as our own
reproductions were not built for

as enough of us drown becoming pronoun:
our bodies have always been matchsticks.

I forget or never knew
       how long and stretched

       and paper thin it gets
       when floating on a sea.

WHAT LASTS ISN'T WHAT'S BUILT TO LAST

until then find quiet, like reciprocity
requires of the wrong skin. the future
is waiting with scenes of uprootedness:

a storm to bowl over this stubborn
stasis held high by the eyes of men
who know themselves best only

when you name them men,
        shapeless & unrelenting &
begging you to know them, even
when you already know their line,

just echoes contorted to rhyme. like promises
kept to the dirt, these men only sow shadows
& shallow roots behind their manmade massifs,
heirlooms designed to know nothing but the sun

and brightly painted watering cans. glittering in
candy apathy and sealed away from rain, these
mountain builders built their own rainshadows
using nothing but nothing but muscles hidden
under the wrong skin

high enough to trap clouds and call it destiny,
high enough to name their work itself as man,
high enough to forget the names of every hand
they twisted to lay bricks of gneiss and granite

     until they lost all sense
     of the old words for rain.
     but root buriers buried deep

     enough to forget new words
     for work, entrusting the sun
     to remember not everything is

     done just because someone has
     done it, like how walls are unfinished
          until they come down.
     not one man will name the rain

when it does come, for it will come,
over the highest mountain and tallest
tales, drowning origin stories watered

with nothing but mountainous echoes.
what are we dreaming when we welcome
the end of the world? something beyond

a fluster of arrogance. are we dreaming
at the end of the world? something
to access after sensation, like
the wrong bodies surviving together.

ON MY BLUE EYES IN A HALL OF MIRRORS

every generation confronts the task
of choosing its past.
    —Saidiya Hartman

condemned & exalted; tumult &
art; horizon & dancefloor; arrested
& passing; conjured & static; static
& static; static & unmagic; static &; static &
locomotion; static & arrested; static & refusal;
refusal & adjacent; & next door; & stacked
one on top of the other, no architecture
ever kept us closer & dancefloor; & beams;
beams & beams; beams & abundance; beams
above & the u-shaped hull; beams & oceans
not seen; beams & branches & beams
from branches; & being; & being
extinguished upwind; & beaten down-
stream from the extinguished; & beams;
& matchsticks; static & sulfur; measured
& traded; brilliance & seduction; & future
waiting in the wings; breathe & concrete;
scene & subjection; future & comedown;
made-up & spotlight; détente & search-

light; & static; static & suspect; scattered
& wretched; uplift & betrayal; & coal;
& diamonds; brilliant & passing; & salvage;
& martyr; martyr & shoulders; martyr
as survival & static; coerced &
confession; & boundary; & witness; condemned
& exalted; to dream & impossible; unbroken
& captured; unwritten & un-written &
static; drowning in horizon & dancefloor
            as tumult & art & canvas, collision

OUR GREATEST AMBITION, TO BE MET SOMEWHERE OTHER THAN THE MIDDLE

passage—just a shadow but sometimes
it's hard to walk around in your own

worn shoes like an old truth, grotesquely
retrospect of addressed flesh & grit

teeth. across a sea that is big & was
already old, what survives may not be

      pretty: what color could shadows be
      once this present gets subsumed?

answered by that familiar hush saved
for spaces where your life is the one

game in town, haunting
you like a ghost that isn't quite

friendly yet carries along with you
knowing you need the company

for the habit of horror.
a habitat teaches you to remain

resilient or alive. most times
that is enough to be, and joy

is safely ignored, but when they demand
to hear mourning you can remain

enough, be made sacred by silence &

leave them to listen & listen & listen
for the stillness of no

sound at all, running head
long for your brilliant, elated pause.

MY MOTHER HAD TO TELL ME

one day I was black and the past
almost let her laugh. She had to

be told, too, but no one ever
bothered so she shared what she had

chance to learn through a life
running: 'they will kill you

if they catch you so you mustn't
let them catch you.' Even now

I say the word us too much
for someone who blends

into so many thems, into a crowd
of our streets and say our names

& syncopated rhythms knowing
equality is the future &

always will be; I say stop killing us
even though I already know

I can always choose to breathe.

If I had been owned by another
time, would I brave marching

to claim my name, choose pride
and right and right and right over

coming fear, coming for the easiest
path—around and not through—

dodging a whole nation plumb
with chimneys' vent, picturesque

curls of smoke, the slow burn
of pain that's learned it's best

delivered patient, returning a body's
investment over handshakes.

most of the time. a black seam,
a coal running endlessly

under every footfall, under a land
in unison, in no rush to know when
it would run out because it would

never run out. I've always had that
chance, a good name and eyes
light enough to choose to see

more than they were seen;
you'd be a fool to choose to be
profit instead of reaping it.

you'd be a fool to even tell
a child he had another way.

I knew I was black when I was
seven years old and only knew

because before seven I knew
I was white. If I was owned

by another time only a fool
would let it slip, like

I had a choice.

"They will kill you if they see you
so you mustn't let them see you."

When I got the talk she made me

promise to remember you can
always be invisible.

FOR ALL THE BROKEN THINGS
UNFIXED WITH NOTHING LEFT
BUT TIME TO FIX THEM

we've discovered whole vocabularies
of disappointment; maybe I am

as old as we all feel, detached
as we all think. what if all this talk

of new normal is nothing more
than old rumor finally hitting the fan
& we all see the very same thing

in inkblot splatters on our separate walls
& can't chalk it up to happenstance, again.

what if all this distance is
a really big mirror facing

the wrong way. what if the universe was not
such an unspeakable terror

for its endlessness & my hands,
pale palms unburned & open,

tumbled each and every one of you
I could ever imagine loving, breathing

& petrified, laying there, waiting, into the inert
vision at the ends of my own

go-go-gadget arms, finally long enough
to fold each and every one

within a single shared thought rather than
only recognizing the universe in deference

to its scale, which we always mistranslate
as endless difference. will each and every

or even just one of you
please pity me with this simple kindness:

tell me it's okay that the universe is so big
that it must be ignored.

ACKNOWLEDGEMENTS

These poems would not be under one cover without the editors who encouraged them along the way, including those at *Autofocus, Crazyhorse, Denver Quarterly, Fence, The Missouri Review, Perhappened, Protean Magazine, Puerto del Sol, Sixth Finch,* and *SocialText,* with a special thanks to the team at Black Lawrence Press, who previously published some of the above in chapbook form.

Further thanks are owed to my parents for giving me more than a mess of pottage, Meir for keeping an eye on the future, and my forever first reader, Molli.